FROM DUST TO DESTINY

The Call : Following God Beyond Familiar Ground

MOHIT SINGH

BlueRose ONE
Stories Matter
New Delhi • London

BLUEROSE PUBLISHERS
India | U.K.

For permissions requests or inquiries regarding this publication, please contact:

BLUEROSE PUBLISHERS
www.BlueRoseONE.com
info@bluerosepublishers.com
+91 8882 898 898
+4407342408967

ISBN: 978-93-7825-321-8

Cover Design: Deepak Katheria
Typesetting: Manisha Rawat

First Edition: March 2026

Dedication

This book is dedicated to:
My LORD and Savior, Jesus Christ:
the Shepherd of my soul,
the Potter of my life,
the Strength in my valleys,
and the Voice that continues to call.

To my Amma (Mom),
my brothers: Pankaj Bhaia and Arun Bhaia,
my dear Bhabhi ji's : Reeta Bhabhiji & Mandeep Bhabhiji whose prayers carried me when my faith was fragile and their support was my strength in valleys.
To my lovely nieces: Anaya & Aarvi.

To every unseen missionary,
every faithful pastor,
every intercessor
who serves without applause.
And to the souls in the Himalayas and beyond,
this journey continues for you.

Acknowledgments

No calling is fulfilled alone.
I am deeply grateful to the many men and women whom God raised in different seasons of my life.

Special thanks to Kumuda Sujay mam, for your hard work in editing this book word by word. I'm grateful!

And Dr. Sushyni Kothuri ji for going an extra mile for proofreading. I'm honored by your presence in this process.

And My dear sister Rhema Grace Syiem for the overall review and grammar check. I'm blessed to have you.

To all dear pastors who are walking with me in ministry with wisdom, humility, and strength. Thank you so much, for trust, covering, and opportunity to serve in Rajasthan, Bengaluru, Punjab, Sikkim, and other parts of India

To all my dear brothers, sisters and friends whose names may not appear here in the book but whose prayers and support remain written in heaven.

To every believer who strengthened me in the Valley of Baka, you were God's springs in my dryness.

Above all, I thank the LORD who never abandoned me in sickness, failure, loneliness, or uncertainty.
This book exists because He stands with me.

Acknowledgments

Author's Note

This book is a personal testimony based solely on the author's lived experiences, reflections, and spiritual journey. It is not written with the intention of criticizing, hurting, or disrespecting any individual, community, religious belief, or cultural tradition.

The purpose of this book is not to promote religious conversion, debate doctrines, or influence anyone's faith practices. It is simply a sincere sharing of personal life experiences and lessons learned through them.

Contents

Introduction

When the Valley Calls Your Name

There are moments in life, when you realize that God's call is not a single event, but a lifelong unfolding.

Some of us imagine calling as a dramatic encounter, a voice from heaven, a clear sign, a decisive moment that changes everything overnight. But for most of us, calling does not arrive like thunder. It grows quietly, like a seed beneath the soil. It stirs in the heart long before it becomes visible in the world.

This book is the story of such a journey.

It is not the story of a perfect man, but the testimony of a faithful God.

It is not the account of uninterrupted success, but of valleys that shaped vision, failures that formed character, and seasons of silence that strengthened surrender.

I was born into a cross-cultural family, raised between different traditions and spiritual influences. From early sickness to academic failure, from internal battles to divine encounters, my life has been marked by questions, tears, and gradual obedience. Yet through every season, one truth remained constant, God was at work.

There were valleys of bitterness like Marah.

There were refreshing springs like Elim.

There were shaping moments in the Potter's house.

There were seasons in the Valley of Baka when tears felt endless.

There were mountains where the clouds hid the future but revealed faith.

And through it all, the call continued.

This book is written for those who are:

- Walking through uncertainty
- Wrestling with calling
- Struggling in hidden seasons
- Serving without visible fruit
- Carrying dreams that feel delayed
- Or sensing a quiet stirring toward something greater

If you have ever asked:

"LORD, are You still working?"

"Does my obedience matter?"

"Is this valley the end?" Then these pages are for you.

I do not write as someone who has arrived. I write as someone still walking. The mountains are still before me. The unreached are still waiting. The lessons are still unfolding.

But I have learned this: God wastes nothing.

Not sickness.

Not failure.

Not loneliness.

Not tears.

Not sacrifice.

Everything becomes part of the shaping.

As you turn these pages, I invite you not merely to read my story, but to reflect on your own.

Where is God shaping you?

Where is He calling you?

Where is He asking you to trust rather than understand?

The Shepherd still calls.

The Potter still shapes.

The valley still refines.

And the call, the sacred, costly, beautiful call: continues.

Let us begin.

Chapter – 1
Childhood in The Valley: Shepherd of My Soul

The sounds that welcomed me into this world were not of silence, but of life: morning religious bells echoing through narrow streets, the murmur of neighbors beginning their day, the distant lowing of cattle, and the rhythm of footsteps on both paved roads and dusty village paths. The air carried the scent of warm earth, cooked rotis, and incense rising with the dawn. Before I ever knew my name, before I could understand direction or destiny, I was already a small lamb placed between two worlds, a city's growing pace and a village's rooted simplicity, held gently in the unseen hands of a faithful Shepherd.

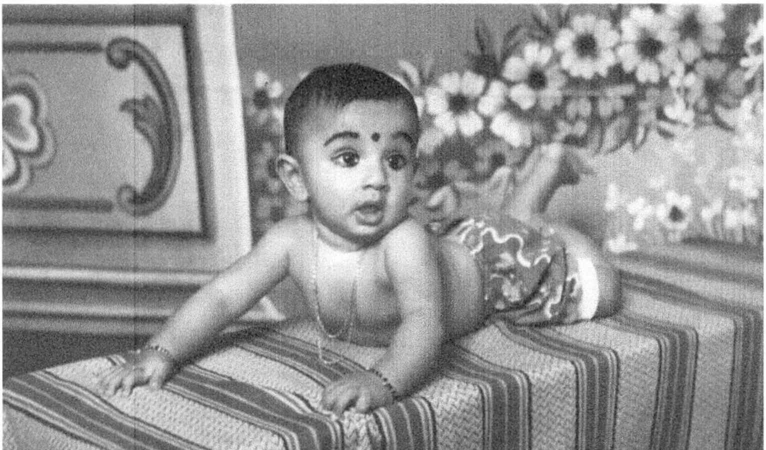

I was born on 6th March 1993 in Jhunjhunu, Rajasthan, a place where the lines between town and village often blur. Life there was neither fully urban nor entirely rural. One moment you could hear the noise of scooters and market chatter; the next, you could see open fields stretching beyond clustered homes, children running barefoot, and elders sitting together under the shade of a tree. My childhood was shaped by both the structured rhythm of city life and the grounded humility of village living. That unique blend formed the soil in which my early years were planted.

I am the youngest of three brothers: Pankaj Singh, the eldest; Arun Singh, the middle one; and then me, the last and the smallest. Being the youngest meant living under layers of affection. I was deeply loved, closely watched, and sometimes overly protected. My brothers had already walked paths I had yet to step on, and I followed behind them like a little lamb trailing stronger sheep, trusting without fully understanding. Their presence gave me security, but even beyond their watchful eyes, another Presence surrounded me.

Looking back now, I see what I could not see then, that the Shepherd of my soul was already guiding my steps. Through the narrow lanes of the town, through village courtyards filled with laughter, through moments of fear, confusion, innocence, and quiet wonder, He was leading me. I did not yet know His voice, but He knew mine. I did not know His plans, but He was already shaping my path.

In that blend of city walls and village skies, I was being formed, protected yet prepared, loved yet quietly led. I was only a child, unaware that every ordinary morning and every simple evening was part of a greater story being written by the Shepherd who never loses sight of even the smallest lamb.

My childhood was not ordinary because my home was not ordinary. I grew up in a cross-cultural and cross-religious family. My mother was from Kerala, a devoted Christian woman whose faith was not loud but steady. My father was a Rajput from Rajasthan, deeply rooted in Hindu tradition and cultural identity. Within one house, two belief systems coexisted. In the same home, incense would burn before idols, and prayers would rise in a devotee's heart. I grew up watching both with the innocent eyes of a child.

As I grew older, a silent question began to form inside me: Whom should I follow? Whom will I be meeting after this life? Who is the true living God? My father's gods and goddesses, or my mother's God, Jesus Christ? No one forced me. No one threatened me. But the tension was real. In Indian society, religion is not merely personal, it is family identity, cultural heritage, and social belonging. Choosing faith can sometimes feel like choosing sides.

So, in my confusion, I did what many children would do, I prayed to both. I would stand before idols and whisper my needs, then I would go quietly and pray to Jesus. But slowly, I began noticing something undeniable. Jesus was answering my prayers. Sometimes the answers came so quickly that it felt as if He had heard my thoughts before I finished speaking. It was not dramatic, but it was deeply personal. I felt seen. I felt heard. I felt pursued.

Without understanding theology, I began experiencing relationships. It was as if a Shepherd was gently calling a lamb by name. I did not know then that my childhood confusion was actually divine training. God was not confused about me, even if I was confused about Him.

In 2004, at the age of eleven, my life entered a deeper valley. I became seriously ill with pneumonia, and what followed was six months of tuberculosis medication. My body weakened. My energy drained. My childhood routine was interrupted by hospital visits and medical treatment. Illness in an Indian household is never just physical; it brings emotional stress, financial concerns, and whispered anxieties among relatives. I remember the uncertainty in the air, the unspoken fear in the eyes of my parents.

I was admitted to Pushpagiri Medical College Hospital in Thiruvalla, a Christian hospital in Kerala. That hospital became more than a medical center; it became a spiritual turning point. Every morning and evening, prayers and worship were broadcast through loudspeakers. The sisters served patients with extraordinary compassion. Their care was not mechanical; it was tender. Lying on that hospital bed as an eleven-year-old boy, listening to worship songs echo through the corridors, something inside me awakened.

I began to believe that if I prayed to Jesus, I would be healed. Isaiah 53:5 says, "By his wounds we are healed." I did not understand the theology of substitutionary atonement, but I believed in healing. Each day, as I prayed, I sensed hope replacing fear. Gradually, I began recovering. Looking back now, I understand that the valley of sickness was not a punishment; it was an introduction. The Shepherd often reveals His voice most clearly when we are too weak to run from Him.

In the Indian context, children are often taught to be strong, to not complain, to endure. But in that hospital bed, I learned that weakness can become a doorway to intimacy with God. The valley was shaping my faith long before I could articulate it.

As my health improved, my spiritual curiosity deepened. During my school years, a simple yet powerful incident strengthened my faith. One day, my best friend told me he was having disturbing dreams and was afraid to sleep. At home, we had only one New Testament shared among the four members of our family. I opened it, tore the last page, and gave it to him. I told him to keep it under his pillow and that the bad dreams would stop. The next day he told me the dreams had ceased.

I was shocked. I had not performed a ritual; I had simply acted in faith. That incident taught me that the Word of God carries power. It was not superstition; it was belief. In that moment, I felt again that Jesus was drawing me closer. Prayer after prayer began to be answered. Slowly, my faith moved from curiosity to conviction.

In May 2010, I got water baptized. It was a public declaration of what had been quietly growing inside me. Yet alongside this growth, I became aware of something unsettling, God was calling me into ministry. I sensed it deeply. But I resisted. I had seen the struggles pastors faced. The Ministry did not look glamorous. It looked sacrificial. It looked uncertain. In Indian society, security is highly valued. A stable career, financial independence, social respect, these are measures of success, but ministry did not guarantee these things.

Academically, another valley was forming. Until Class 9, I performed well. But my 10th board results shook my confidence. In 11th and 12th, I shifted from RBSE to CBSE and chose Science with Mathematics, believing it would secure my future. My English was weak. The syllabus was difficult. The pressure was intense. In Indian homes, board exams carry enormous weight. They are seen as stepping stones to dignity or shame.

I remember sitting in a chemistry class, overwhelmed by anxiety, and making a silent contract with God: "If you help me pass in my 12th class, I will come for full-time ministry. Just help me." It was a desperate bargain made out of fear.

When the results were announced, my friend checked them for me. His voice was heavy when he said I had failed in two subjects and was required to take a compartment exam. My heart sank. Telling my mother was one of the most painful experiences of my life. She understood before I finished speaking. Tears filled her eyes. At that moment, I felt like I had failed not only an exam but my family's expectations.

The weight of failure in Indian society is crushing. Relatives ask questions. Comparisons begin. Internal shame grows. Dark thoughts entered my mind. I wondered if my future was finished. I questioned

Jesus. I reminded Him of my promise. I wondered why he had not intervened.

But slowly, through the silence, I sensed God exposing something deeper in my heart, pride. Somewhere inside, I believed I could succeed without fully surrendering to Him. The failure was not rejection; it was refinement. I later cleared the compartment exam, but the lesson remained. Today, I hold multiple degrees, including two bachelor's degrees and one master's, and I am pursuing another master's in English literature. Yet I will never forget the boy who failed 12th grade. That failure became foundational. It broke my self-reliance and deepened my dependence on the Shepherd.

When I shared my desire to enter ministry, my family resisted. My mother loved me deeply and dreamed of a secure future for me, perhaps engineering or defense services. In our entire generation, no one had become a pastor. Ministry seemed like a path of suffering. Bible college admission dates passed, and I had to wait one year. That year felt painful, but it became preparation. Under the guidance of my Pastor, I served and gained experience. The Shepherd was shaping my character quietly.

Through all these experiences, God began teaching me through the metaphor of sheep and shepherd. Jesus calls Himself the Good Shepherd in John 10. In ancient times, shepherds-built enclosures and slept at the gate so that nothing could enter without passing through them. I realized that throughout my life, the Shepherd had stood at the gate. Illness, failure, depression, none of it reached me without His permission. He was not absent in my valleys; He was present at the entrance.

Sheep do not plan tomorrow's pasture; the shepherd does. Matthew 6 reminds us not to worry about tomorrow (Matthew 6:31, 32 - "So do not worry, saying, 'What shall we eat?' or 'What shall we drink?' or 'What shall we wear?' For the pagans run after all these things, and your heavenly Father knows that you need them").

When I thought my academic failure had destroyed my future, the Shepherd already knew the path ahead. He knew I would pursue higher education. He knew the calling he had placed on my life.

Jeremiah 29:11 "For I know the plans I have for you," declares the Lord, "plans to prosper you and not to harm you, plans to give you hope and a future." It shows that God has plans for hope and a future. My life is evidence that setbacks are not accidents; they are redirections.

Sometimes sheep climb mountains and become stuck, unable to move forward or backward. Spiritually, I too became stuck between ambition and surrender. Yet the Shepherd kept calling, "Come to Me." Like a creator who knows how to repair what He made, Jesus knew how to restore my broken confidence.

A shepherd provides measured provision, using his staff to pull down branches but not cutting the entire tree. God gives blessings according to our capacity. Sometimes He withholds some things to protect us. Sometimes He allows pain to strengthen us.

1 Corinthians 10:13 assures us that He will not allow more than we can bear ("No temptation has overtaken you except what is common to mankind. And God is faithful; he will not let you be tempted beyond what you can bear. But when you are tempted, he will also provide a way out so that you can endure it."). My failure, my waiting season, my delayed entry into ministry, all were measured by His wisdom.

The shepherd also uses his rod to correct sheep from eating poisonous plants. Correction in my life, through failure and delay, was not cruelty; it was love. Genesis 2 shows God setting boundaries for Adam. Boundaries are expressions of care. In the same way, God corrected my pride and redirected my path.

Above all, the Shepherd's heart is filled with emotion:

- John 10:11 declares that the Good Shepherd lays down His life for the sheep ("The thief comes only to steal and kill and destroy; I have come that they may have life, and have it to the full. I am the Good Shepherd. The good Shepherd lays down his life for the sheep.").
- Luke 15 reveals that He leaves the ninety-nine to seek the one. (Luke 15:4 "Suppose one of you has a hundred sheep and loses one of them. Doesn't he leave the ninety-nine in the open country and go after the lost sheep until he finds it?")

- Isaiah 40 portrays Him carrying lambs close to His heart. (Isaiah 40:11 "He tends his flock like a shepherd: He gathers the lambs in his arms and carries them close to his heart; he gently leads those that have young.").
- Psalm 23 promises comfort even in the presence of enemies. Throughout my childhood valleys, He was not distant; He was deeply involved.

As I look back at my childhood in the valley, I see that nothing was wasted. The cross-cultural tension, the sickness, the academic failure, the family opposition, and the waiting season were all part of divine shaping. The Shepherd used my background, my breakdowns, and my battles to bring me closer to Him and to His purpose.

To every reader who feels trapped in a valley, whether of family conflict, illness, academic disappointment, or emotional breakdown, hear this truth: the valley is not your end. It is often where the Shepherd introduces Himself most intimately. Your failure is not final. Your pain is not pointless. Jesus, the true Shepherd, uses every experience to shape your destiny and draw you into deeper faith.

My childhood was not a story of perfection but of pursuit. The Shepherd pursued me through sickness, through confusion, through pride, and through pain. And as this chapter closes, one truth remains clear: the valley prepared me for the voice. The voice that would soon stir my soul. The voice that would call me beyond comfort into purpose.

For when the sheep finally recognizes the Shepherd's voice and chooses to follow, a new journey begins. And that journey leads into the next chapter: The Call: The Stirring in the Soul.

Chapter – 2
The Call: The Stirring in The Soul

"Your career is what you're paid for. Your calling is what you're made for." - Steve Harvey

"Now to him who is able to do immeasurably more than all we ask or imagine, according to his power that is at work within us." - Ephesians 3:20 (NIV)

While the valley of my childhood was the place where the Shepherd found me and guarded my fragile faith, this chapter marks the season when His voice began to resonate with unmistakable clarity. The protection of the Shepherd gradually gave way to the shaping of the Potter. The One who had shielded me from destruction was now forming me for direction. What began as a gentle awareness evolved into a holy unrest within my spirit, a stirring that would not allow me to remain ordinary.

There are seasons in life when comfort becomes heavy. Outwardly, nothing dramatic seems to change. You continue your studies; you fulfill family responsibilities. You laugh with friends, internally, something deeper is shifting. It feels like standing before a door you cannot see yet, but somehow know it exists.

The heart whispers questions: "Is this all?" "Was I made for something more?" That was the condition of my soul. The thought of ministry did not descend suddenly. It emerged slowly, like the dawn piercing darkness. At first, it was a faint impression, then it returned repeatedly and eventually, it settled into conviction. Ministry was no longer a distant idea; it was personal summons.

I understood that obedience required preparation. If I were to serve effectively, I needed equipping through training. Bible college became not simply an aspiration but an act of surrender. Yet I must confess that my early desire to enroll carried both spiritual hunger and personal insecurity. I was painfully aware of my weakness in English. Academic settings had exposed my limitations. Words faltered when I most needed clarity. I longed to grow, not merely for academic success, but to communicate truth with confidence and grace.

God often begins His deepest work through our weaknesses. What we perceive as inadequacy becomes the very ground where calling takes root. My insecurity about language became the doorway to greater dependence. What began as a practical decision matured into spiritual obedience.

When I first spoke to my family about the call I sensed upon my life, their response was not opposition but concern wrapped in love. As the youngest son, I was deeply cherished. They had seen ministers who travelled far from home, facing financial uncertainty, cultural barriers, and emotional fatigue. Their questions emerged from care:

"How will you sustain yourself?"

"What kind of future will you have?"

"What about security?"

In a family where no one had ever stepped into pastoral ministry, this path appeared uncertain and unfamiliar. In our context, stability is often equated with responsibility. Career decisions are not merely personal choices, they reflect family identity and honor. I understood their hesitation. Yet the stirring within me intensified rather than diminished.

During the year of waiting that followed, I found myself suspended between two worlds. I was encouraged to apply for engineering colleges and even consider the defense services. I purchased application forms and I held them. I tried to imagine myself wearing a uniform or building a career in engineering. Those paths promised dignity, stability, and social recognition. Yet every time I attempted to fill out those forms, my heart resisted. My hands hesitated. It felt as though I would be betraying something sacred within me.

That year became a crucible. I wrestled internally with obedience and expectation. I did not want to walk into ministry by wounding my family's trust. Their blessing mattered deeply to me. I prayed fervently that God would soften their hearts if this calling was truly from Him.

Slowly, in His time, permission came. Their words were cautious: "Do not blame us later. This is your decision." Yet beneath their caution lay love and surrender. They released me, even though they did not fully understand the path ahead. With gratitude and trembling faith, I stepped forward.

Entering the Potter's House

Under the guidance of my pastor, I enrolled at Northern Institute of Biblical Studies in Patiala, Punjab, for a Bachelor of Theology (B.Th.). The first day humbled me profoundly. When a teacher instructed me to bring a chair and sit down, I could only stare back in blank confusion, unable to understand. My weakness in English was publicly exposed. Shame rose quickly. For a moment, I questioned whether I belonged there.

Yet humiliation can either cripple or cultivate. That moment awakened resolve. I became determined that I would grow, not for pride, but for purpose. I immersed myself in learning English and Punjabi. I embraced the culture and the people of Punjab with affection and respect. Ministry opportunities opened in local congregations. I preached, observed, learned, and served. Theology ceased to be theoretical; it became embodied in community life.

Simultaneously, with permission from the college administration, I enrolled in a Bachelor's program in Philosophy and Psychology through IGNOU. Intellectual curiosity and spiritual formation progressed together. The stirring in my soul did not subside; it deepened.

The Vision of the Mountains

In my final year of B.Th., as we prepared to choose ministry placements, I entered a season of fasting and prayer. I asked God sincerely, "Where do You desire me to serve?" During one such time of prayer, I experienced a vivid inner impression. I saw the map of India, and my attention was drawn toward regions near Bihar, Nepal, and China. A red mark appeared and slowly moved toward the Himalayan regions, touching India, Nepal, Tibet, China, and Bhutan.

The image unsettled me. Mountains signified remoteness, difficulty, unfamiliar terrain. I resisted inwardly. I prayed honestly: "Lord, send me to places where life is easier, UK, USA, Canada. My family would rejoice. The path would be smoother." Yet the vision persisted. The stirring refused to fade. I carried that image silently within my heart.

Calling often disrupts comfort. It invites us beyond preference and into purpose. Like Jeremiah, who felt unprepared because of his youth, I felt inadequate. But the Potter was shaping vision within me before shaping the assignment.

Deeper Formation: M.Div.

Desiring greater theological depth, I applied for M.Div. at SABC in Bangalore. Financial realities confronted me. The fees were significant, and uncertainty lingered. I questioned how it would be possible. Yet once again, my mother and brothers stood beside me. Their financial, emotional, and spiritual support strengthened me immensely. I had always desired to pursue ministry with their blessing. Their partnership affirmed that God's shaping extended beyond me to my family.

Bangalore introduced new dimensions of growth. Academic rigor intensified. Spiritual disciplines deepened. There were nights of loneliness, moments of doubt, seasons of spiritual dryness. Yet each struggle became a tool in the Potter's hands.

THE POTTER'S HOUSE

Jeremiah 18 describes a prophet observing a potter at work. The imagery is simple yet profound. The Potter shapes intimately. His hands are involved. The clay is not an accident; it is intentional material chosen for design.

My calling journey unfolded through three aspects of the Potter's work: the Wheel, the Hand, and the Way.

1. *The Potter's Wheel*

The wheel represents movement, constant, deliberate, purposeful. Even when the clay appears unchanged, the wheel is turning. During my waiting season, during academic humiliation, during financial uncertainty, the wheel was moving.

When I failed my 12th grade, I believed everything had stopped. Yet years later, as I completed multiple degrees and preached before respected leaders, I realized that the wheel had never ceased. God's work continued in unseen ways.

The wheel's movement signifies that transformation requires rotation. Comfort prefers stillness, but calling requires motion. Every turn removes excess pride. Every spin reshapes perspective. Every revolution aligns destiny with divine design.

If the wheel were to stop, it would suggest abandonment. But the One who shapes neither sleeps nor grows weary. His purposes persist through our confusion and clarity alike.

2. *The Potter's Hand*

Jeremiah 18:4 reveals that when the clay was marred, the potter reshaped it as seemed best to him. The clay was flawed, but not forsaken. The potter's hand subjects clay to water, pressure, sunlight, and fire. Water softens resistance. Pressure molds structure. Sunlight dries fragility. Fire strengthens endurance.

My life encountered each stage. Academic embarrassment softened pride. Financial constraints molded dependence. Loneliness dried superficial confidence and cultivated inner resilience. Internal struggles became refining fire.

Pain is not always punitive; it is often preparatory. Just as muscles ache in development, spiritual maturity requires discomfort. Pain awakens attention. It exposes areas requiring surrender.

Others may evaluate your life superficially, like analyzing a cake by ingredients and price. But only the Creator understands the intention and emotion behind the formation. Only the Potter sees the final vessel in His imagination before it exists in reality.

Limited perspectives attempt to define identity, but the Potter's hand defines destiny.

3. The Potter's Way

The Potter's way is patient, redemptive, and purposeful. He does not discard flawed clay. He reshapes. He forgives. He continues working. Past failures do not intimidate Him. Just as Paul transformed from persecutor to chosen vessel, broken narratives become testimonies in the Potter's design.

The Potter responds to posture. Some resist shaping because it is painful. Some fear the vessel they might become. Some crack under pressure and refuse to return to the wheel. But others surrender and whisper, "Here I am. Shape me."

Submission is trust, trust that the fire will not exceed capacity, trust that the vision in the Potter's mind surpasses personal ambition. My responsibility has been to remain available. Clay does not argue; it yields. Formed from dust and destined to return to dust, I desire to remain useful until my final breath.

From Stirring to Shaping

The stirring that began quietly in the valley matured into surrender in the Potter's house. Calling demanded patience, humility, perseverance, and faith. It required releasing imagined futures and embracing unseen mountains.

Heartbreak, loneliness, financial challenges, cultural adjustments, all became instruments in divine hands. They were not obstacles but shaping tools. The Potter used every tear, every doubt, every delay to refine my character and clarify my purpose.

If you sense a stirring within your soul, do not suppress it. The path may stretch you beyond comfort. It may challenge expectations, but the One who calls is faithful to shape. He wastes nothing, not your pain, not your waiting, not your weakness.

The Shepherd who protected me in the valley became the Potter who formed me for purpose. And though shaping continues, I stand assured that every spin of the wheel is guided by loving hands.

The journey now moves forward, into seasons where valleys and peaks will intertwine.

Chapter – 3
The Wilderness: Between Marah and Elim

"Cast all your anxiety on Him because He cares for you." - 1 Peter 5:7

"God is not asking us to understand His ways, but to trust His heart." - Helen Roseveare

"God is looking for people through whom He can do the impossible. What a pity that we plan only the things we can do by ourselves." - A. W. Tozer

Life with God is not a straight line. It is a pilgrimage marked by peaks and valleys, by moments of breathtaking clarity and seasons of unsettling silence. There are times when we stand on spiritual mountaintops, where vision is clear, strength feels abundant, and the sense of divine purpose is undeniable. And then there are valleys: low places where the air is thick with uncertainty, where prayers seem to linger unanswered, and where obedience does not immediately yield visible fruit. My journey has carried me through both landscapes.

Marah and Elim

Scripture offers a vivid portrayal of this spiritual rhythm in the wilderness journey of Israel: *Marah and Elim* (Exodus 15:22–27). After the dramatic victory at the Red Sea, where God displayed His power in a way that no generation could forget, the Israelites entered the Desert of Shur. For three days they traveled without water. When at last they found water at a place called *Marah*, it was bitter and undrinkable. The very thing they longed for became a source of disappointment. Relief turned into frustration, and celebration gave way to complaint.

Marah represents those seasons when what you expected to refresh you instead wounds you. It is the place where obedience feels costly and outcomes feel bitter. It is where faith is tested not by enemies, but by silence. Yet *Marah* was not the end of Israel's story. After *Marah* came *Elim*: twelve springs of water and seventy palm trees. Abundance followed bitterness. Shade followed exposure. Rest followed testing. In my own life, *Marah* and *Elim* have not been abstract concepts; they have been lived realities.

After completing my Bachelor of Theology, I found myself in a season of uncertainty regarding my vocational direction. I chose to teach in a school for a year. I poured myself into the lives of children, preparing lessons, encouraging growth, investing relationally. Outwardly, it was meaningful work. Inwardly, something felt unsettled. A persistent question echoed within me: Is this where I am meant to remain? It was not rebellion against God, nor was it dissatisfaction with the children. It was a subtle tension, a sense that I was functioning, but not flourishing in my particular calling.

That quiet unrest was my first *Marah* in ministry. Nothing was overtly wrong, yet the water did not taste sweet.

Marah often disguises itself as stability. It looks safe. It appears reasonable. But internally, it carries a bitterness that reveals misalignment. The dissatisfaction I felt was not ingratitude; it was divine prompting. God was not condemning my work; He was reminding me of my specific calling.

Financial uncertainty added another layer of testing. Ministry, especially in its early stages, does not always come with visible provision. There are moments when you wonder whether your obedience is truly aligned with God's pleasure. Questions rise quietly: Am I doing this in a way that honors Him? If I am, why is the provision delayed? Why does it feel so fragile?

At *Marah*, Israel grumbled because they forgot the Red Sea. They focused on the present bitterness rather than past faithfulness. I recognized the same tendency within myself. When resources seemed limited, my focus shifted from gratitude to calculation. I began measuring rather than trusting.

But in the wilderness, God revealed His character. He declared Himself Jehovah Rapha, the LORD who heals. He promised covenant faithfulness. *Marah* became a place not only of testing but of revelation. God was not merely providing water; He was forming trust.

After completing my Master of Divinity (M.Div.) from SABC, Bengaluru, I returned to Rajasthan with a specific burden for youth ministry. I joined a church and began traveling to universities. I preached to young minds hungry for direction. I mentored students navigating identity and purpose. Those days felt purposeful. There was movement, growth, and engagement.

Then 2020 interrupted everything. The pandemic shut down gatherings and restricted travel. Universities were empty. Church activities were halted. In that quietness, I began writing blogs and reflecting more deeply. I considered turning my experiences into a book, though at that time the project did not materialize. It felt like sowing seeds into some hidden soil.

The pandemic altered the landscape of the world. In that uncertain environment, I applied for a position in an international process at Amazon. I was selected and worked there for six months. I was earning a good pay. It was dignified employment, structured and reliable. I learned discipline and responsibility in that environment. Yet each day

I sensed a deeper disconnect. It was as though I was walking efficiently but in the wrong direction.

Marah does not always appear as dramatic suffering. Sometimes it is simply the absence of visible fruit. It is the tension between effort and outcome. It is the internal battle of remaining faithful when no one sees.

In January 2021, I received a call to plant a church in Bangalore under New Life Fellowship Trust. During the Zoom interview, I openly shared that after two years I sensed a calling to the mountains. From a practical perspective, it was unusual to appoint someone for such a defined period. Yet they agreed. Looking back, I see God's hand guiding that arrangement.

I stepped into church planting during active lockdown restrictions. The first year was profoundly challenging. Week after week, I prepared sermons, prayed fervently, and reached out to people. Yet the visible response was minimal. When people asked how the ministry was progressing, I often felt a silent ache. There were no impressive numbers to report. There were no dramatic testimonies to share.

That year was my deepest *Marah.*

The water was there, but it was bitter. I learned to preach without visible affirmation. I learned to trust that unseen seeds were taking root. I learned that fruitfulness is not always immediate.

Exodus tells us that at *Marah,* Moses cried out and prayed to the LORD. God showed him a piece of wood, which he threw into the water, and the water became sweet. I often reflected on that moment. The solution was not discovered through human strategy but divine instruction. Bitterness was transformed not by complaint but by obedience.

In my own *Marah* season, the "wood" was prayer. It was surrender. It was choosing to remain where God had placed me despite discouragement.

Then, in 2022, *Elim* arrived, when lockdown restrictions eased, something shifted in the atmosphere of the church. People began coming from various states, such as: Bihar, Nagaland, Andhra Pradesh, Rajasthan, Tamil Nadu, Karnataka, Kerala, Maharashtra, Odisha, and West Bengal. By Christmas, more than seventy individuals were gathering. Professionals, doctors, engineers, lawyers, managers, nurses, became part of the community.

It was not merely numerical growth; it was spiritual confirmation. The same ground that once felt barren began to produce life.

One incident remains deeply personal. I fell ill during that season. A believer who was a doctor at a major hospital reached out with concern and care. At that moment, I reflected on the previous year when I felt alone and unseen. God had been preparing people long before I recognized their arrival.

Elim is not a self-created success. It is divinely timed refreshment.

Yet *Elim* carries its own test. At *Elim*, the danger is not bitterness but complacency. Before blessing, God tests perseverance. After blessing, He tests gratitude. Will we remain humble when provision flows? Will we remember that the springs are gifts, not achievements?

Throughout these seasons, another battle intensified within me, the war between facts and opinions. Opinions whispered, "You are ineffective. You are not called. You have failed." These voices often grow louder in *Marah*. But facts rooted in God's Word declared something different: "You are chosen. You are called. You are my workmanship."

Biblical history reveals this tension repeatedly. Sarah relied on human reasoning rather than divine timing. Job endured suffering while clinging to the truth. Daniel faced lions yet trusted God's sovereignty. Peter faltered under public pressure but later stood boldly anchored in revelation. Circumstances do not redefine identity. God's truth remains constant.

As my two-year commitment in Bangalore neared completion, the burden for the mountains intensified. An option was presented to continue under organizational covering while relocating. It was secure and structured. Yet internally, I sensed God inviting me into deeper trust.

I returned home to Rajasthan and spent three months preparing my mother's heart for my departure. Those days were tender. A mother's concern is not easily quieted. I carried both conviction and compassion within me. I prayed earnestly, asking God where He would lead me, Kathmandu (Nepal) or Gangtok (Sikkim).

Then a call came from my dearest friend and brother, Ps. Pawan Tamang regarding an opportunity in Gangtok, Sikkim. A video conversation followed with Ps. Samuel Subba. As we spoke, peace settled deeply within me. There were no dramatic signs, only quiet assurance.

On 11th August 2023, I arrived in Gangtok, Sikkim. I knew no one personally. There were no visible guarantees. Yet there was unmistakable peace.

I realized then that safety is not found in visible security but in obedience to God's leading.

Marah taught me dependence. *Elim* taught me gratitude. *Marah* revealed my weakness. *Elim* revealed God's faithfulness. In *Marah*, prayer deepened. In *Elim*, praise expanded.

Today, if you are in *Marah*, do not assume you have reached the end. *Marah* is a place of testing, not termination. Cry out rather than complain. God reveals sweetness in response to surrender.

If you are in *Elim*, remain humble. *Elim* is a resting place, not a permanent dwelling. Gratitude protects the heart from pride.

Life with God will continue to alternate between valleys and peaks. Both are part of the shaping process. Both prepare us for a deeper trust.

Marah and *Elim* are not contradictions; they are companions on the journey of faith. They teach us that God is present in bitterness and in abundance, in silence and in celebration. As we cast our anxieties upon Him and choose to trust His heart rather than our understanding, we discover that neither valley nor peak defines us. Our Faithfulness in response to God's faithfulness does.

And the journey does not end here. Beyond *Marah* and *Elim* lies another unfolding, where the lessons of testing and refreshing will converge into something greater than personal growth.

The story continues.

Chapter - 4
Legacy in The Clouds

"God's work done in God's way will never lack God's supply." - Hudson Taylor

There are seasons in ministry when you find yourself standing on a mountain wrapped in clouds. You know you are elevated, yet your vision is limited. You sense purpose, yet you cannot see the entire path. You look ahead, and the future is concealed. You look behind, and the journey feels distant. In such moments, you realize something profound: legacy is not written in visibility. It is written in trust.

When I reflect upon my life and the call, I do not see a story of uninterrupted triumph. I see seasons of provision and seasons of pressure. I see nights of quiet prayer where no one else knew what I was carrying. I see tears that never made it to public testimony. But above all, I see something unmistakable, God raising people.

Time after time, when the weight felt heavier than my capacity, when resources seemed insufficient, when loneliness whispered discouragement, God sent individuals. Not as angels descending visibly from heaven, but ordinary people moved by extraordinary grace. I have learned that God's supply rarely drops from the sky untouched. It passes through human hands.

There were moments when the needs seemed simple on the surface but carried deeper emotional strain. A practical example of God's attentiveness occurred during a season when my phone started malfunctioning. In ministry, communication is not a luxury; it is a lifeline.

Counseling, prayer requests, sermon preparation, coordination everything flowed through that small device. As it began to fail, I felt a quiet frustration. I researched new options privately. I checked stores discreetly. I examined installment plans. I kept this struggle private because I did not want to appear dependent.

But while I was calculating, God was orchestrating.

Church leadership felt moved to provide a new phone. Around the same time, Shreyas (My brother and dearest friend) approached me with an offer, completely unaware of my silent struggle. I remember sitting alone afterward, overwhelmed. It was not about the device. It was about divine attentiveness. God had seen what I had not spoken. It was His tenderness.

On another occasion, I prayed specifically for a tablet. I needed it for study, sermon organization and delivery, digital ministry, and research. I did not make it a public request. On my birthday, Shreyas surprised me with that exact gift. I held it with gratitude that went far beyond technology. It was covenanting faithfulness manifested in human generosity.

There was also a digital watch I had prayed for, not as ornament, but as a practical tool during travel and ministry scheduling. Noel and Akila from Bangalore blessed me with it. A laptop, which I once considered beyond reach, was also provided through their love. Each provision felt like a whisper from heaven: "You are seen and loved."

Ultimately, these provisions taught me a lesson that far transcended technology; they showed me the beauty of spiritual partnership.

Bangalore church family became a living expression of God's faithfulness through every season. Jean and John strengthened me with their wisdom and presence. Vijender brother and Martha sister offered counsel that matured my ministry perspective. Ps. Sam Varghese and Blessy Chechi became anchors of encouragement. Ps. Shibu and Litty sister, Esther, Samson, Shyni, Nelson, Maya, Ps. Samlal, Ps. Sam Skaria, Ps. Luke, Ps. Charles, Ps. Gopi, Aunty Somey, Ps. Jason Immanuel, Vandana sister, Sumit brother, Subhash brother and Mary sister, Neelambari sister, Ashish bhaia, each name represents more than assistance. They represent God's faithfulness embodied.

In difficult seasons at Sikkim, Katherine, Ps. Ruben and her family stood with me in unwavering support. Gerald and Reinhild became pillars of support when discouragement pressed heavily.

Iaishan, his mom and his family from Shillong embraced me as their own. Their commitment was not convenience; it was conviction. They counted me as part of the family.

In Sikkim, I remain profoundly grateful for Ps. Swapan K. Biswas, chairperson of Mashi Mandali Ministries. Under his leadership, doors opened in ways I could never have engineered. Ministry in unfamiliar terrain demands covering, discernment, and spiritual fatherhood.

Through him, God provided more opportunities to multiply God given gifts and talents.

When I consider these relationships, I see more than kindness. I see the Valley of Baka.

Psalms 84:5–7 declares:

"[5] Blessed are those whose strength is in you, whose hearts are set
on pilgrimage. [6] As they pass through the Valley of Baka, they make
it a place of springs; the autumn rains also cover it with pools. [7] They
go from strength to strength, till each appears before God in Zion."

The Valley of Baka is not clearly marked on any map. The Hebrew root suggests weeping, like resin dripping from a tree, resembling tears. It symbolizes dryness, sorrow, exhaustion. Psalm 84 was sung by pilgrims journeying to Jerusalem. They walked long distances. They crossed arid valleys. They faced fear and scarcity.

The Valley of Baka represented the hardest stretch of the journey.

Yet Scripture says something extraordinary: as they passed through, they made it a place of springs.

They did not avoid the valley.
They did not pitch permanent tents in sorrow.
They did not allow dryness to define them.

They transformed the valley.

The psalm reveals three eternal principles:

FIRST: God blesses us from strength to strength.

The text says they go "from strength to strength." Not from comfort to comfort, but from strength to strength. Strength is forged in tension. Even in dryness, God provides rain. Even in exhaustion, God provides pools.

The Valley of Baka today may look like emotional burnout. It may look like loneliness in ministry. It may look like unanswered financial questions. It may feel like preaching without response or serving without recognition.

Yet if your strength is in the LORD, the valley becomes testimony. Tears become wells.

David understood this. Hunted by Saul, hiding in caves instead of ruling in a palace, betrayed instead of honored, his life resembled a Valley of Baka. Yet he wrote, "You have kept count of my tossings; put my tears in your bottle" (Psalm 56:8). His tears did not evaporate; they were recorded. His psalms still refresh hearts centuries later.

In the Bible, Ruth endured widowhood and uncertainty in a foreign land. Yet faithfulness in famine placed her in a lineage of redemption. Hannah wept in barrenness, misunderstood and mocked, yet her tears birthed Samuel, a prophet who would anoint kings.

Valleys did not erase their destiny. Valleys prepared it.

<u>SECOND</u>: We are blessed to be a blessing.

Psalm 84 says, "They make it a place of springs." Rain represents divine grace. But someone had to dig the ground to hold the water. Human obedience partnered with divine provision.

This is a ministry: sometimes you dig wells you may never drink from. Sometimes you labor in obscurity so someone else may flourish in visibility. I recall entering spaces that were neglected, cleaning and preparing quietly so others could worship freely. No one applauded the preparation. But worship flowed.

Joseph's life illustrates this. Betrayed by brothers, sold into slavery, falsely accused, imprisoned, years of silence. Yet when famine came, he became provision not only for Egypt but for his family and to the then known world. What appeared as delay was divine design.

Job endured catastrophic loss. Wealth gone; Children gone; Health deteriorated; Reputation questioned, yet he chose not to curse God. In the end, he prayed for those who misjudged him, and restoration followed. Brokenness refined him.

<u>THIRD</u>: You will be a blessing after you have gone through the valley.

In the Valley of Baka, your words carry weight. If they cannot heal, silence may be wiser. You never know the silent battles someone fights. Every servant of God walks through dry terrain.

There were moments when I hesitated to help others because I feared misinterpretation. I did not want generosity to be seen as surplus. But God gently corrected me. Obedience matters more than perception. Giving is not about proving capacity; it is about reflecting Christ.

Pain reveals character.

Cain allowed rejection to become violence. Saul allowed insecurity to become hostility. Jonah allowed disappointment to become resentment. The elder brother allowed comparison to harden his heart.

The Valley of Baka exposes what resides within.

Our Ministry is not immune to heartbreak. Loneliness visits unannounced. Financial strain tests conviction. Misunderstandings wound deeply. But I have seen this truth: those who strengthen others in their valley are themselves strengthened by the LORD and they strengthen others.

The individuals who stood beside me during fragile seasons were not diminished; they were fortified. As they refreshed others, they were refreshed.

The Valley of Baka is never permanent. Scripture says, "As they pass through." They pass through. Hard seasons have expiration dates. God's faithfulness does not.

When I arrived in Sikkim, uncertainties surrounded me. New language rhythms. New culture. Limited structure. Few visible guarantees. Yet peace anchored me. And in that season, God began sending people, each like a spring in arid terrain.

Legacy in the clouds is not about recognition. It is about obedience in obscurity. It is about trusting that God builds through community. It is about recognizing that answered prayers often wear human faces.

Some blessings are developmental, not demonstrative. Some provisions are confirmations, not conveniences.

If you are in your Valley of Baka, do not interpret silence as absence. The valley may be shaping you to carry water for many. If you are in abundance, remember that springs are entrusted to you for distribution.

Ministry is sustained not by charisma but by covenant. Not by self-sufficiency but by shared faithfulness.

As I look at the tapestry of names woven into my journey, I see orchestration. I see rain filling pools dug in tears. I see God transforming isolation into partnership. I see strength rising from surrender.

And I know this: those who strengthen others in the valley go from strength to strength.

The clouds that once limited vision now feel like witnesses. They testify that God never abandons His servants. He surrounds them, with people, with provision, with purpose.

The journey continues. The calling deepens. The legacy is still being written, not in applause, but in faithfulness.

Beyond these clouds lies further obedience.

Chapter Five: The Call Continues.

Chapter – 5
The Call Continues

"I will go anywhere, provided it be forward." - David Livingstone

"How, then, can they call on the one they have not believed in? And how can they believe in the one of whom they have not heard? And how can they hear without someone preaching to them? And how can anyone preach unless they are sent? As it is written: 'How beautiful are the feet of those who bring good news!'" - Romans 10:14- 15 (NIV)

As the call continues in the heart of the Himalayas, I often find myself standing on the balcony of my room in Bojoghari, Gangtok, watching the clouds move across the mountains. The weather here can change within minutes. One moment, the sky is clear and the peaks are visible in majestic detail. The next moment, everything disappears into mist.

In many ways, that has been my life.

When I first arrived in Gangtok, I was both excited and overwhelmed. The air felt different. The language rhythms were different. The cultural nuances were different. The weather itself was shocking. Cold winds, sudden rain, dense fog, it felt as though even nature was testing my resolve.

For the first year, I stayed in a homestay. It was simple, quiet, and unfamiliar. The following year I shifted to Taktse Seda. In both places, God placed me under landlords who were not merely kind but godly. I began to understand that divine provision is not always dramatic; sometimes it is the quiet placement of safe spaces.

The call becomes more manageable when you are not walking alone.

In Sikkim, Ps. Samuel Subba, whom I lovingly call Daju and Lydia Bhawju accepted me not as an outsider but as family. There is a profound difference between working under someone and belonging with someone. Daju did not merely allow me to assist in ministry; he stood with me as a supportive elder brother. Whenever I received invitations to preach in other churches, he encouraged me. When decisions weighed heavily, he guided me. When I felt uncertain, he reassured me.

Leadership without insecurity is rare. And I remain deeply grateful.

In Bojoghari, I was blessed to walk alongside pastors from ten churches united under the United Christian Fellowship (UCF). Under the leadership of Ps. Sager Rai, there was unity that transcended individual platforms. I was added to the core team of the youth wing of these ten churches.

Through youth meetings, church services, counseling sessions, and teaching opportunities, God expanded my understanding of collaborative ministry.

Ministry is about people, not platforms.

Over the past two and a half years in the mountains, I have been involved in youth ministry, church ministry, counseling, preaching, and teaching. Some days were filled with visible fruit. Other days were heavy with unseen battles. Through every season, one truth became clearer: God is active in every phase of life. He guides. He protects. He provides.

Provision is not always material. Sometimes it is mental stability when anxiety tries to overwhelm you. Sometimes it is emotional strength in the midst of heartbreak. Sometimes it is the unexpected gift of a bike that makes ministry travel possible. Sometimes it is the courage to preach when your heart is breaking.

One of the most painful experiences of my ministry occurred during a trip to Putharjhora. I had been invited by Ps. Prakash Gurung and his church team for a ministry program. Before that, I had spent time in Shillong with Iaishan and his family, who had embraced me as their own. From there, I traveled to Putharjhora. The three days of ministry were blessed and meaningful.

But on the journey back to Sikkim, tragedy struck.

One of our cars fell from a cliff.

Four members of our team lost their lives instantly.

There are moments in life when language fails. Standing at the funeral service that Sunday, looking at coffins of those who were laughing and serving beside me just days earlier, I felt something inside me shatter. I was asked to preach. My heart was broken. My mind was clouded. My emotions were numb.

Yet I preached.

Not from personal strength, but from divine grace. That day, I learned something profound: some days in the mission call are sustained purely by God's strength. There is no emotional reserve. There is no intellectual preparation that can carry you. There is only surrender.

That experience stripped away any illusion that I had a lot of time for ministry. It reminded me that life is

fragile. Calling is urgent. Obedience cannot be postponed.

God did not keep me confined to the mountains.

God did not keep me confined to the mountains. In 2024, He opened a door for me to travel to Indonesia for Evangelism Explosion (EE) training. There, I learned to share the Gospel more effectively. I met men and women who were passionately committed to the harvest field. It expanded my vision. It strengthened my confidence. It reminded me that the call is larger than geography.

Yet calling comes with a cost.

Let me speak honestly about the ministerial journey.

There is financial uncertainty. There are months when provision feels delayed. There is emotional loneliness, even when surrounded by people. There is the tension of choosing calling over comfort. There are waiting seasons where results are invisible. There are moments when trusting God defies human logic. There are hidden spiritual battles that no one sees behind public ministry. There are misunderstandings and criticism. There is the daily guarding of purity and character.

The call is beautiful, but it is not easy.

However, there are blessings when you remain faithful.

There are unexpected provisions. There are divine appointments. There are people God sends precisely in critical seasons. There are miracles that strengthen faith. There is deep inner rest even in chaos. There is calmness in uncertainty. There is freedom from comparison. There are resources that arrive at the right time. There are lives transformed. There are youth redirected. There are families restored. There are seeds planted for generations.

And there is confidence, quiet unshakeable confidence that you are in the perfect will of God.

As I reflect on the continuation of this call, my heart is drawn to the life of Miriam, the sister of Moses.

Exodus 15:20–21 tells us:

"Then Miriam the prophet, Aaron's sister, took a timbrel in her hand, and all the women followed her… Miriam sang to them: 'Sing to the LORD, for he is highly exalted.'"

But Miriam's story did not begin at the Red Sea. It began in slavery.

Israel had endured four hundred plus years of bondage. Their hearts were dulled. Their bodies were weary. Their hope was fragile. Miriam was born into the harshest period of servitude.

She was a daughter of Jochebed, from the tribe of Levi. Her name carries complexity, associated with bitterness and rebellion.

She understood bitterness intimately.

She watched oppression. She witnessed suffering. She saw her baby brother placed in a basket on the Nile. Yet she did not collapse into hopelessness. When Pharaoh's daughter discovered Moses, it was Miriam who stepped forward and said, "Shall I go and get one of the Hebrew women to nurse the baby for you?" (Exodus 2:7).

She understood her responsibility in the moment.

From Miriam's life, I draw four lessons that have shaped my own journey:

FIRST: Hope

Exodus 3:7 declares that God had seen the misery of His people and heard their cry. Miriam believed that. Though surrounded by slavery, she carried hope. She knew the stories of Abraham, Isaac, and Jacob. She knew that God remembers.

In my first year of ministry in BTM, Bangalore, when nothing seemed to grow, hope carried me. I had no visible fruit, but I had conviction that God remembers.

Micah 6:4 reminds us that God sent Moses, Aaron, and Miriam. She was part of divine strategy. Even in slavery, God was preparing deliverance.

Hope sustains calling.

SECOND: Preparation.

Many scholars believe the women carried timbrels out of Egypt because they anticipated deliverance. They prepared instruments during exile. They believed that one day they would worship freely.

Are we preparing for the miracles we pray for?

When I was in seasons of obscurity, I studied deeply. I pursued further degrees. I prepared sermons when no one was listening. I trained myself when platforms were limited. Preparation is faith in action.

Like two farmers praying for rain, one prepares the soil; the other does not. Whose faith is stronger? The one who prepares.

THIRD: Understanding responsibility.

Miriam recognized her role. She was not Moses, yet she was vital for her ministry to the women of Israel. When she stepped forward and led women in worship, they followed her. She inspired faith in the wilderness.

Leadership is not always front-facing; sometimes it is formative.

In ministry, I have learned to recognize moments where stepping forward matters. Whether in youth meetings, counseling sessions, or crisis situations, responsibility cannot be ignored.

FOURTH: Learning from wrong choices.

Numbers 12 records a painful episode where Miriam and Aaron spoke against Moses. The LORD heard it. Miriam was struck with leprosy and isolated for seven days.

But what matters is repentance and restoration. Moses cried out, "O God, please heal her." And she was healed.

We all have a past. But the question is: are we repeating it, or learning from it?

"We do not grow with experience, but with evaluated experience." - John C. Maxwell.

If someone speaks of your old mistakes, ask yourself: am I still that person? If you have changed, you are not defined by yesterday. Every saint has a past, but every transformed life has a future.

Miriam's life teaches humility over grumbling. The first generation of Israelites missed the Promised Land due to unbelief and complaining. The call requires humility.

As I conclude this book, I carry a burning desire: to see Jesus lifted high in the Himalayan region. To reach these regions and beyond. To reach unreached communities. There is more I cannot write here. But the call continues.

If you are reading this, perhaps you sense a stirring in your own heart. Perhaps you are in your Valley of Baka. Perhaps you are in *Marah.* Perhaps you are in *Elim.* Perhaps you are being shaped in the Potter's house.

Wherever you are, do not abandon hope.

Prepare even in exile.

Understand your responsibility.

Learn from your mistakes.

Do not grumble, be humble.

God remembers.

Malachi 3:16 says that those who feared the Lord spoke with one another, and the Lord listened, and a scroll of remembrance was written.

He remembers, and as long as he remembers, the call continues.

The clouds may conceal the mountains, but they cannot erase them.

The call continues.

And so does my obedience.

Epilogue
The Journey Is Not Finished

When I began writing these pages, I did not intend to present a perfect story. I intended to present a man who was and is trying hard to follow the call.

This book is not the record of a man who never struggled. It is the testimony of a man who was carried. It is not the story of uninterrupted victories, but of valleys that shaped vision. It is not the narrative of someone who always understood God's ways, but of someone who slowly learned to trust His heart.

From childhood in a cross-cultural home, to sickness and healing, from failure in academics to surrender in calling, from *Marah*'s bitterness to *Elim*'s refreshment, from the Potter's shaping hand to the Valley of Baka's tears, and finally to the continuing call in the Himalayas, every season has whispered the same truth: God remembers.

There were days when I questioned the path. There were nights when loneliness pressed heavily. There were seasons when results were invisible. There were moments when heartbreak shattered comfort. There were misunderstandings, hidden battles, and sacrifices that few saw.

But through it all, the Shepherd never abandoned His sheep.

The Potter never stopped turning the wheel.

The valley never had the final word.

Looking back, I realize something profound: the call of God is not a single event; it is a continuous unfolding. It is not a moment at an altar or a decision in youth. It is daily obedience. It is waking up when you are tired. It is praying when you feel dry. It is preaching when your heart is broken. It is trusting when the road ahead is unclear.

The call continues not because we are strong, but because JESUS is faithful.

If you are reading this and you find yourself in a valley, do not lose heart. The valley is not permanent. It is a passage. If you are standing on a peak, remain humble. The peak is not the destination either. It is a preparation for deeper surrender.

Perhaps you sense a stirring within you, a quiet call that will not fade. Perhaps you are afraid of what obedience may cost. Let me tell you gently: the cost is real. But the grace is greater.

Ministry is not about platforms; it is about people. It is not about recognition; it is about redemption. It is not about comfort; it is about calling.

The mountains still stand before me. The clouds still move across the Himalayan sky. The unreached still wait. The youth still search for direction. The broken still long for hope. And so, the call continues.

Romans 10 asks a question that echoes across generations:

"How can they hear without someone preaching to them? And how can they preach unless they are sent?"

If no one goes, how will they hear?

If no one speaks, how will they believe?

If no one obeys, how will the Kingdom advance?

The Great Commission is not a suggestion. It is a command from the LORD, and each of us must respond.

For me, that response led to deserts and mountains, to loss and laughter, to tears and testimonies. And if the LORD grants me breath tomorrow, it will lead me further still.

Perhaps to Nepal.

Perhaps to Bhutan.

Perhaps beyond borders yet unseen.

Wherever it leads, I pray only this: that I may go forward.

As David Livingstone once said, "I will go anywhere, provided it be forward."

If you remember anything from these pages, remember this:

Do not grumble, be humble.

Do not fear, have hope.

Do not delay, prepare.

Do not compare, obey.

God remembers those who fear Him. Malachi tells us that a scroll of remembrance is written before Him for those who honor His name.

Your faithfulness is never unnoticed.

The Shepherd still calls.

The Potter still shapes.

The valley still transforms.

The springs still flow.

And the call, the sacred, unstoppable, life-giving call : continues.

Until the day we stand before Him in Zion, going from strength to strength (Psalms 84:7). Amen.

About the Author

Mohit Singh is a pastor, teacher and missionary currently serving in the Himalayan region of India. Born in Jhunjhunu, Rajasthan into a cross-cultural family, his life journey has been shaped by faith, struggle, surrender, and obedience.

After completing theological (B.Th. & M.Div.) and secular studies (B.A. & M.A.) and serving in various ministerial contexts across India, he sensed a strong calling toward the mountains. He now serves in Gangtok, Sikkim, actively involved in youth ministry, church ministry, preaching, teaching and counseling.

His heart burns to see the Gospel reach unreached communities across the Himalayan belt and neighboring regions. Through personal testimonies and biblical reflections, he seeks to inspire believers to trust Jesus in every season, from valleys of bitterness to mountains of purpose.

Instagram and Facebook Scanner:-

@MOHIT_SINGH_SOLANKI_

Email Id.:- mohitsingh.88888@gmail.com

About the Book

Shaped in the Valley.

Called to the Mountains.

Strengthened in the Clouds.

From childhood sickness to academic failure.

From desert seasons of bitterness to unexpected springs of provision.

From church planting struggles to missionary calling in the Himalayas.

This deeply personal spiritual memoir traces one man's journey through:

- The Shepherd's protection
- The Potter's shaping hand
- Marah's testing and Elim's refreshment
- The Valley of Baka's tears
- And the continuing call beyond comfort.

With honesty, theological depth, and pastoral warmth, this book reminds readers that: God remembers.

Valleys are passages, not prisons.

Brokenness is preparation.

And the call never truly ends.

If you have ever questioned your calling, walked through spiritual dryness, or wondered whether obedience is worth the cost, this book will strengthen your faith and reignite your hope.

The journey is not finished.

The call continues.